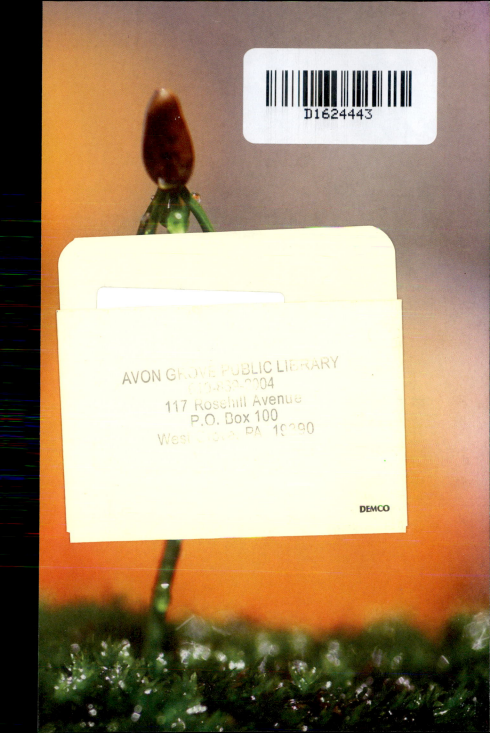

Wetlands Journey

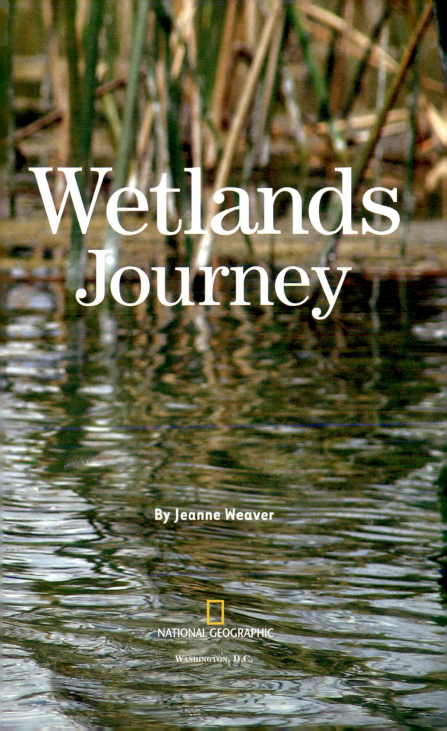

Wetlands
Journey

By Jeanne Weaver

NATIONAL GEOGRAPHIC

WASHINGTON, D.C.

Founded in 1888, the National Geographic Society is one of the largest nonprofit scientific and educational organizations in the world. It reaches more than 285 million people worldwide each month through its official journal, NATIONAL GEOGRAPHIC, and its four other magazines; the National Geographic Channel; television documentaries; radio programs; films; books; videos and DVDs; maps; and interactive media. National Geographic has funded more than 8,000 scientific research projects and supports an education program combating geographic illiteracy.

For more information, please call
1-800-NGS-LINE (647-5463) or write to the following address:

National Geographic Society
1145 17th Street N.W.
Washington, D.C. 20036-4688
U.S.A.

Visit us online at www.nationalgeographic.com/books

For information about special discounts for bulk purchases, please contact
National Geographic Books Special Sales at ngspecsales@ngs.org

For rights or permissions inquiries, please contact National Geographic
Books Subisidiary Rights: ngbookrights@ngs.org

Copyright © 2007 National Geographic Society

Text revised from *Better Off Wet* in the National Geographic Windows on Literacy program from National Geographic School Publishing, © 2004 National Geographic Society

All rights reserved. Reproduction of the whole or any part of the contents without written permission from the publisher is prohibited.

Published by National Geographic Society. Washington, D.C. 20036

Design by Project Design Company
Photo Editor: Annette Kiesow
Project Editor: Anita Schwartz

Printed in the United States

Library of Congress Cataloging-in-Publication Data

Weaver, Jeanne.
  Wetlands journey / by Jeanne Weaver.
      p. cm. – (National Geographic science chapters)
  ISBN 978-1-4263-0185-8 (library)
  1. Wetland ecology–Juvenile literature.
  2. Wetlands–Juvenile literature. I. Title.
QH541.5.M3W337 2007
577.68–dc22

2007007789

Photo Credits
Front cover: © Klause Nigge/National Geographic Image Collection; Spine, Endpaper, 2-3, 9 (top), 14, 16, 19, 21, 24, 26 (top), 27, 32: © Shutterstock; 6: © Chris Johns/National Geographic Image Collection; 8: © Mattias Klum/National Geographic Image Collection; 9 (bottom): © Raymond Gehman/National Geographic Image Collection; 10, 17: © National Geographic Image Collections; 11: © APL/Minden Pictures; 12: © Richard Hamilton Smith/CORBIS; 13: © Naturfoto Honal/CORBIS; 15: © National Geographic/Getty Images; 18: © Joe McDonald/CORBIS; 20: © Jeff Vanuga/CORBIS; 22: © Yogi, Inc./CORBIS; 23: © Nigel J. Dennis; Gallo Images/CORBIS, 25: © Nature Picture Library; 26 (bottom): © Anthony Bannister; Gallo Images/CORBIS; 28: © Charles Philip Cangialosi/CORBIS; 30: © Raymond Gehman/CORBIS; 31: © Kevin Fleming/CORBIS; 34: © Daniel Cox/Getty Images; 35: © Katja Kreder/Jupiterimages.

Endsheets: Tiny water droplets cling to moss and moss spore capsules.

Contents

Welcome to Wetlands

Can you guess what a wetland is? It is an area of land that is soaked with water. Wetlands are like huge sponges. The soil in a wetland soaks up water. Many kinds of plants and animals live in wetlands.

There are different types of wetlands. Some wetlands are very large. Some are very small. A wetland can be beside a river, lake, or ocean. A wetland can be a low spot in the woods or in a field. Some wetlands have trees. Others have grassy plants.

◄ Newborn American alligators rest on their mother's head in the swampy wetlands of the Florida Everglades.

In this book, you will visit a damp, spongy wetland called a bog. You will also see a swamp. A swamp is a wetland with trees. Next, you will explore a grassy wetland called a marsh. Your journey ends with a trip to one of the most amazing wetlands in the United States—the Everglades. So, put on your rubber boots and let's go!

In the cool, still evening air, a foggy bog with its shrubs and decaying moss looks eerie.

Some swamps look like forests growing out of a smooth layer of water.

Grasses and floating water lilies grow in the marshes in Yellowstone National Park in Wyoming.

The moss helps support the trees in a watery bog. A walkway protects the moss from hikers.

Chapter 1

Bogs

When walking in a forest, you might find a wetland called a bog. Bogs are areas of wet ground that are covered with plants. The plants soak up the water and make the ground spongy.

Tiny green plants called sphagnum moss grow in bogs. The moss grows thick like a carpet. When you stand on the thick moss, it jiggles and sways beneath your feet.

Like a sponge, sphagnum moss absorbs and holds water.

Cranberries float in a bog in Wisconsin. Bogs are common in the north-central and eastern United States.

Sometimes a bog looks like a field in the forest. But watch out! What looks like solid ground may be plants floating on water.

Only a few types of plants grow in bogs. The soil and water do not have the nutrients most plants need to grow.

One plant that can grow in a bog is a cranberry plant. The cranberry plant is a long tangle of green leaves and roots that spread over the water.

The insect-eating sundew plant does not need nutrients from soil. It is a bog plant that has sticky red hairs to catch, hold, and slowly digest insects.

Bog Life

The bog is home to frogs, snapping turtles, insects, and a few birds. Other animals come to visit. They live in forests and other areas around a bog.

One animal that doesn't mind getting wet is the beaver. The beaver has an oily coating on its fur. When it comes out of the bog, water drips off its fur. The beaver is soon dry.

Long hair and a thick, oily coat keep the beaver warm even in icy waters.

A snowshoe hare can hop on its big feet just minutes after it is born.

The snowshoe hare lives near bogs and nibbles on the plants that grow there. It needs little to drink and gets most of its water from the plants it eats. The snowshoe hare has big feet shaped like snowshoes and is a fast runner. It can race across the moss in a bog without sinking into the water.

Cypress trees grow tall in the swamps of southeastern United States. Here the weather is warm and there's plenty of rain.

Chapter 2

Swamps

A swamp is a wetland that has woody plants like shrubs and trees. Swamps may dry out at times during the year. Cypress trees grow in swamps. They have special roots for swamp living. Cypress tree roots spread out far from the tree. This helps keep the tree stable in the soft, muddy ground.

Some of the cypress trees' roots rise back up out of the water. Roots (circled) that do this are called "knees." Scientists thought knees supplied other tree roots with oxygen from the air. Today they are not sure and are doing more research.

Swamp Life

A swamp is full of small animals like crayfish, frogs, and water beetles. A crayfish looks like a small lobster. Crayfish can survive when the swamp is dry because they can dig into the soil to find water.

Many different kinds of frogs live in and around swamps. There is plenty of food in swamps for frogs. They eat insects, worms, and slugs.

A crayfish gets ready to defend itself against predators in its swampy habitat.

The bullfrog's color helps it blend in with its surroundings.

Diving beetles also live in swamps. These beetles dive underwater for food. They eat snails and tiny fish. Diving beetles have a space under their wings to hold air while they are underwater.

An American alligator is black with a rounded snout, powerful jaws, and horny scales along its back. Waiting for prey, the alligator often floats with only its head above water.

Big animals live in and around swamps. Alligators live in swamps. These animals are large and dangerous, but they are a big help in a swamp.

When a swamp begins to dry up, the alligator digs a deep hole in the mud. This "gator hole" fills with water. During dry weather, turtles, shrimp, and fish live in the gator hole. There would be very few fish in a swamp without gator holes.

Three Florida redbelly turtles sun themselves on swamp plant stems.

A great blue heron makes its home in
the marshes of Kings Bay in Georgia.

Chapter 3

Marshes

A marsh is a wetland where grassy plants grow. Marshes can be found beside a river, lake, or ocean. Like a swamp, a marsh can be wet part of the time and dry part of the time.

Unlike a bog, the soil in a marsh is rich in nutrients. This means that many different kinds of plants can grow there.

A bird has built its nest in the cattails.

Cattails and reeds grow in marshes. A cattail is a tall, narrow plant that can grow between 4 feet (1 meter) and 9 feet (3 meters) high. Cattails can soak up lots of water and store it in their roots and stalks. Cattails are home to many types of birds and animals.

Cattails grow at the edge of a marsh.

Wading birds, such as this great blue heron, have long legs and wide feet to help them walk through a marsh.

Marsh Life

Lots of birds live in marshes. A marsh is a good home for the great blue heron. The heron wades in the shallow water on its long legs while it hunts for fish. Its long neck and beak allow it to snatch up a meal from the water.

A great white egret takes flight from wetlands in southern Florida.

Snails and other small animals living in the marshes are food for migrating birds.

26

A flock of migrating avocets fly over marshy wetlands.

In the fall, many birds migrate, or travel, south to warmer areas. In the spring, the birds migrate north again. The grassy plants in a marsh make a resting place for migrating birds. Great white egrets stop to rest and feed. They eat fish, frogs, snails, and all kinds of insects.

Chapter 4

Protecting the Wetlands

Wetlands provide homes and food for many different plants and animals. But they do a lot for people, too. People used to think wetlands were not important. Now we know better!

Wetlands help to prevent floods. The spongy ground and plants in a wetland soak up extra water when there are heavy rains. Areas with wetlands nearby have little flooding.

◄ An airboat carries visitors through Everglades National Park.

Schoolchildren explore the Barn Island Marshes, restored wetlands along the coast of Connecticut.

Wetlands help keep our drinking water clean. Sometimes, waste from farms or factories pollutes the water. The polluted water is soaked up by the plants and thick soil in a wetland. When this happens, some of the pollution is taken out of the water.

People Change Wetlands

Wetlands help people. Yet people harm wetlands. People move to wetland areas. They dig out and drain the land to build homes, roads, and shopping centers. They pollute the air and water.

These activities destroy wetlands. They make it hard for plants and animals to survive. This is what has happened to one of the most unusual wetlands in the United States—the Everglades, in Florida.

Many wetlands have been taken over for housing developments such as this one built on the coastal edge of the Everglades.

A black-necked stilt rests on one leg in a wetland pond in the Everglades.

The Everglades

The Everglades is a large area of marshes, swamps, and open water in southern Florida. Here water moves slowly over the soggy land like a river. Grassy plants called sawgrass cover large parts of the wetland. The Seminole Indian tribe calls the Everglades Pa-hay-okee, which means "grassy water."

Cypress and mangrove trees also grow in the Everglades. Herons, egrets, and other birds wade in the water or nest in trees. Large manatees swim through deeper water. The Everglades is full of life.

Protecting the Everglades

The Everglades was once twice as big as it is today. Long ago, the Everglades covered about 11,000 square miles (29,000 square kilometers). Then people started moving to southern Florida. They drained water from the wetland. They used the land for farming and to build towns. Many plants and animals lost their habitats and were in danger of becoming extinct, or dying out.

The Everglades

The Everglades National Park is home to the Florida panther and other endangered species.

Finally, one person spoke up. Marjory Stoneman Douglas wrote a book called *The Everglades: River of Grass*. It said the Everglades was important for animals and people. Many who read this book agreed. They made officials listen. Laws were passed to help the Everglades.

Today, the Everglades still has some of the same problems. But some people are trying to save and restore the wetlands. There is much more to be done to help the Everglades.

It is important to protect wetlands. Many animals and plants rely on them for their homes. People need wetlands because they help to prevent floods. They keep water clean. Wetlands are better off wet!

From the boardwalk, visitors look at unusual plants and wildlife protected in the Big Cypress Swamp in the Everglades.

How to Write an A+ Report

1. Choose a topic.
- Find something that interests you.
- Make sure it is not too big or too small.

2. Find sources.
- Ask your librarian for help.
- Use many different sources: books, magazine articles, and Web sites.

3. Gather information.
- Take notes. Write down the big ideas and interesting details.
- Use your own words.

4. Organize information.
- Sort your notes into groups that make sense.

- Make an outline. Put your groups of notes in the order you want to write your report.

5. Write your report.

- Write an introduction that tells what the report is about.

- Use your outline and notes as you write to make sure you say everything you want to say in the order you want to say it.

- Write an ending that tells about your report.

- Write a title.

6. Revise and edit your report.

- Read your report to make sure it makes sense.

- Read it again to check spelling, punctuation, and grammar.

7. Hand in your report!

Glossary

bog an area of wet, acidic, spongy ground

endangered plants or animals that may become extinct because there are so few of them living today

extinct no longer living

flood water overflowing onto dry land

habitat areas where an animal or plant usually lives

marsh watery ground where grasses grow

migrate to move from one place to another

nutrient food that makes plants and animals grow

oxygen a gas in the air that plants and animals need to live

pollute to make dirty

predator an animal that eats other animals

prey an animal that is hunted or eaten by other animals

sphagnum a type of moss that holds water, also known at peat moss

swamp watery land where woody plants like trees and shrubs grow

wetland an area of land that is soaked with water

Further Reading

• Books •

George, Jean Craighead. *Everglades*. New York: Harper Trophy, 1997. Grades 2–4, 32 pages.

Kalman, Bobbi, and Amanda Bishop. *What Are Wetlands?* (Science of Living Things Series). New York: Crabtree Publishing, 2002. Grades 2–4, 32 pages.

Marx, Trish. *Everglades Forever: Restoring America's Great Wetland*. New York: Lee & Low Books, Inc., 2004. Grades 3–6, 48 pages.

Stille, Darlene R. *Wetlands* (True Books–Ecosystems). New York: Children's Press, 2000. Grades 2–4, 48 pages.

• Web Sites •

Miami Museum of Science
http://www.miamisci.org/ecolinks/everglades

National Park Service
http://nps.gov/ever/forkids/index.htm

ThinkQuest
http://library.thinkquest.org/J003192F

U.S. Environmental Protection Agency (EPA)
www.epa.gov/owow/wetlands

U.S. Fish & Wildlife Service
www.fws.gov/nwi/educator.htm

Wisconsin Department of Natural Resources Environmental Education for Kids
http://dnr.wi.ov/eek

Index